March Book

March Book

Jesse Ball

Grove Press
New York

Published simultaneously in Canada
Printed in the United States of America

Grateful acknowledgment is made to the editors of the magazines in which these poems first
appeared:
New Republic: "After a Death"; The Paris Review: "March Book," "Cares," and "Secret
History of Jacques Rennard"

FIRST EDITION

Library of Congress Cataloging-in-Publication Data
Ball, Jesse, 1978–
    March book / Jesse Ball.
        p. cm.
    ISBN 0-8021-4122-6
    I. Title.
PS3602.A596M37 2004
811'.6—dc22   2003067628

Grove Press
841 Broadway
New York, NY 10003

04 05 06 07 08   10 9 8 7 6 5 4 3 2 1

For Robert, Catherine, and Abram Ball

CONTENTS

FOREWORD

I suppose (though I no longer *remember*) that at twenty-five one may have ac-
tually lived a life of thrilling and terrible adventures like those in young Mr. Ball's
book, which is significantly named for the month when Spring begins—*real-
life adventures*, we longingly called them, reading about these actions and pas-
sions in the novels of Sir Walter Scott or Robert Louis Stevenson.

But it now seems to me far more likely that such derring-do and the discourse
pertinent thereto—

> . . . For memory's sake,
> drive slowly along the avenue of my name, and call
> at every number, saying *Jesse,*
> *there are fifteen rules for every day, and you, you fool,*
>
> *you've broken every one,* saying, *Jesse,*
> *we've come to take you,*
> *we've come at last to take you where you need to go.*

is more likely to be the product of a finely focused imagination, fueled to some
degree by fictions like those I have mentioned, or even by such veracious nar-
ratives as *Travels in Arabia Deserta* or other errancies in sufficiently outlandish
locales. I am sustained in my quest for plausibility by the overtones of a fabu-
lous past in most of Jesse Ball's poems, the resonance of Once-upon-a-time so
likely to make its presence felt in the work of a young poet (think of Keats, if
that is not too daunting an instance). And surely *this* young poet concedes as
much in the close of his "Self-Portrait as Brueghel's Beekeepers"—

> . . . their father sits them down in a ring at night
>
> and tells stories while they tremble, not bearing
> to touch one another for fear they will be stung.
> What perfect letters they must write . . .
>
> Were I the one to whom this letter came,
> I'd keep it folded in my coat
> as proof of the world I imagine.

But I stipulated a focused imagination, which is not that state of mind, or of *being*, which can be achieved by reading old books. A better indicator of visionary gifts is indeed vision, what the poet *sees* and makes us see through his eyes. And such observation is persistently and vehemently there, or at least invoked, from the very first line of these poems—"And now we see"—and throughout thereafter: "you saw passing / processions of that which might / have been the holy," "strange to see the search end here / at the edge of the fairground," "we should all see differently, though of course / some do, some are made to do," "if strange animals mourn countries we cannot see / then listen when they mutter," "one could see in the distance the unreal bulb of a water tower," "in a glass / we have stood to be seen, gone / in the quiet to places we could not understand," "pair your child with a swan / and have other animals see openly / this intimate act of favoritism," "observe that someone has altered the scenery. / No longer can we look out on the world we had hoped for."

In all these citations, as in many others later in the book, vision is one term of a dialectic with what will not or cannot be seen: to observe something is to posit what escapes observation. This is the tension that generates most of Jesse Ball's poems, and it is a fruitful anxiety.

Of course, no one writing in our moment, when so much has been taken away, can escape the toils of modernity, even a poet so young as Jesse Ball, even one so receptive to the rhetorics of old time. Why else would there be so distinct a temptation of prose—such a high prose quotient—contesting (as I see it) these remarkable verses? For it is prose which persists, which continues until it leaches into the sands of discourse and disappears, just as it is verse which ceremonially returns (*reverses*), recuperating its formal commitment until it establishes vision as the visionary. That there should be such a proportion of prose in this poet's work (which is, however, never prosaic) is the index of a struggle for "the sacred truths" he has had to wage against the exactions of his moment. It is a tally of his triumph that he can versify the question of his combat in this high fashion:

> Who among us can name his home,
> can speak without fear, and stand
> resolute outside the haze of his own life
> when the mountains come,

disguised as horsemen, sending
their weight in waves before them
shuddering over the cold ground?

May it be an appropriate close to this responsive note if I cite the young poet's engaging *mea culpa* ("The failure of modernity . . . has brought us to many horrible passes"), which is "A Speech" he makes in front of a curtain, costumed, precisely, as the young poet obliged, he acknowledges, to speak in prose if in his own person:

. . . the only books we know are the ones that we ourselves wrote. They will be no help to us, just as we ourselves can be no help to each other. If someone were to forgive me for the things I did in my youth, even that would be an affront. Those crimes are the only evidence that I have lived.

—Richard Howard

But now thou dost thyself immure and close
in some one corner of a feeble heart.
—George Herbert

1

ABOVE A STREET

And now we see that your permissions
and the great banners of your admittance
are lost in the midday fog.

Your coat is forgotten in the workroom;
your umbrella, nose down, was set in a stand
from which you had not the time to retrieve it.

For through the window you saw passing
processions of that which might
have been the holy, clad in feasting

gowns, replete with bells, indiscriminate
with cheer, fingers fat with rings,
heads bowed beneath plain cloth,

and so you ran out in the noon street,
shirtsleeves rolled, and hurried after
that which might have passed.

Strange to see the search end here,
at the edge of the fairgrounds,
on a day when there's no fair.

You look around, shocked again
that your life continues to proceed
in fragments that couldn't possibly

add up to anything. Whatever
you thought you saw, it's gone now.
You must walk back along the avenues

as a fierce sun resumes the work
of morning, burning through fog
bit by bit, until there's nothing between you

and the suddenness of age, nothing between
your life and the blued violence
of the burdened, calamitous sky.

SELF-PORTRAIT AS BRUEGHEL'S BEEKEEPERS

In the foreground, a beekeeper pauses on a slope.
Another will soon pass him. Behind them, bees,
other beekeepers, a tree and in it a man, legs wrapped

around a branch. There's the building
where they sleep, the baskets in which they keep
the hives, as if it were possible, this life with bees.

None of them has a face, not even beneath their woven
helmets. If they have hands, then those
rarely go ungloved. One wonders what they talk about

during long evenings. It's plausible to think
they were never children, but simply arrived one day
on the fringes of this place and took up their tasks,

seamlessly, with no recognition that things had not always
been thus. Equally plausible: they are children,
and their father sits them down in a ring at night

and tells stories while they tremble, not bearing
to touch one another for fear they will be stung. What perfect
letters they must write, hazarding news, stray thoughts:

The bees in the south pasture grow in number. They sense
cold days coming, and if they speak or gather, as once they used to do,
then they do it now in secret, in places to which we cannot go.

Were I the one to whom this letter came,
I'd keep it folded in my coat
as proof of the world I imagine.

INSIDE THE STOVE

Inside the stove, he found
a passageway, leading to a set of stairs.
This caused him a great deal of worry
as well as elation and gladness of living.
He did not, however, venture
into the oven, but sent his little brother in
in his stead. This seemed at first
a good idea, but when the brother
had been gone three days, he began
to second-guess the wisdom
of his rash choice. He'd go in after him,
he decided. But the passage
had shrunk by then, and no normal-sized
person could fit through. Yes, that's it,
I sent him in because, from a purely physical
standpoint, I myself could never have gone.
And besides, he mumbled to himself,
it's probably nice in there.

AFTER A DEATH

His wife waits by the gate. The afternoon meal
is all but finished. What will you say to her,
which of the speeches, long prepared, will fall

trippingly from your tongue?

The village center's just a short walk. The parson
is a clever man, and fancies himself a puppeteer.
You watched him play out Luther's amazement

with a small stringed toy. Still, the point is made.

We should all see differently, though of course
some do, some are made to do. So it seems,
Lynn, so it seems (and here you pause,

thinking better). Well, let's go for a walk.
I've been inside all day. The train must have been
dreadful. But nice to leave the city?

Lynn's clothing is severe. She speaks

using her hands, and says she didn't expect
any of it to happen. It's just chance,
the chance we take. Yes, you say,

yes, Lynn. We took it. And you don't, or can't,

touch even her arm. And she won't, can't,
grimace, laugh. It happened on a roadway,
you say, in a German landscape. All of a sudden,

where God wasn't, God was. We should be so lucky.

The ottoman stands for servitude.
The pearl earrings, desired purity.
The set of jacks means hope spurned.

The medicine chest: ambiguous.
It could and does mean
any number of things, like statuary.

Clocks bespeak a morbid
fascination with death. Candles
mean callow intervention, laughter.

The curtains are altruism,
the martlet, loss. The shrouded
piano is all too obvious:

anticipation. The film of the faena
and the looped recording of the fado
by the blind have meaning in sorrow

or something like it, since sorrow
itself stands for mastery, and mastery
for wounding. It's all very

confusing, and is, of course, why we
receive guests in the garden, and never
let them enter our house.

NO. 31, CONFLICT WITH A GOD

1.

Somehow, I'd always thought
the swans were watching me.

(When it broke through the underbrush,
great wings wild with the sun,

I was delirious and didn't think to run.)

2.

Act begets act. Pinned
beneath him in the grove,

I gave Helen to a world of suitors.
Too many suited her. The city fell

the day she burst from that egg.

3.

Still, I might have dropped
the baby down a rural well,

or taken my own life.
At the god's approach

the ground rang like a bell.

4.

I might have asked him
something as we fell.

So many things need answers.
But his feathers were cold, near metal.

Though soft, he hurt to hold.

5.

His eyes are everywhere—
truth, even if it isn't true.

They say all of a god's strength
is *mind*. The physical gives way.

I was the world, burst in a day.

DIPLOMACY

The ambassador comes, and it seems like a parlor trick,
one that's a little frightening, for which the children
are dismissed from the room. The unease that's wed
to the sleight of hand should fade, the cruelty
fall away in a welter of smiles. But no one can smile.
The linden tree creaks beyond the farthest windows
of this enormous house. Delegates line the walls,
sternly dressed, coats buttoned to the throat,
monocles, spectacles glaring. Hands trained to stillness
are immeasurably still. The ambassador ascends the stairs
with a racket of hooves. The door swings open,

and he is in the room. A threat clings to his skin,
to his lupine eyes, to the taut veins of his shorn skull.
He settles his long coat over the back of a chair
and turns with a hideous bow to address the quorum.
All his motions seem to proceed from a stretching
of limbs that ought not to do the things
they are called upon to do. Everyone can feel it:
the ambassador is insane. And yet, and yet
they have sent him to barter at this late hour,
when the slightest chicanery, the hint of a fist,
is certain death for everyone involved.

CEDAR HILL

Those raised near deep water understand
death as drowning, understand the lost as drowned.

Patience is inherited, bred in centuries that overlook the sea,
in cemeteries, cramped houses, safe harbors.

Tired of such rooms, such doors, I believe
I am sick of human thresholds. Out in the yawning fields

the only danger is the horizon. How it shifts and dances,
how it trails after like a dog with a secret.

If strange animals mourn countries we cannot see,
then listen when they mutter.

Any hint might be a help to we who have no help.

CARES

In winter, we take a cottage on the long bay.
The north wind breaks shutters and moves
through the riddled hulks of Victorian gravesites,
where the still light etches the marrow

of our limbs in marriage. By this strait, the moon
is measurably close. It prefers such places, drifts of water,
old windows, rooms in which the wicked sleep.

Anna, I say, are the terms right? For we
will have many a cold hour in these syllables.
This north land keeps quiet, beneath
truths the sun forgot during many passages,

many erring lives of emperors. We shall learn
the hazards, the wagers, the systems of martingale,
all hours in the rigid March sky. For we are young

and newly come from confidences of the south.
We are young, and we—my bride, myself—
have decided not to know anyone, not to know
any people anymore. For there are circles

within circles, and just as I stitch another
month into a gravid year, Anna has poured
what we care for into a bowl. She will stir it,

standing by the open door in the thinnest of dresses,
a dress so thin I needn't touch her to know
that of all the things in the world, this is the one
thing we were told we could never have.

The failure of modernity, said the man in the black coat, is the failure of the machine to act morally. It never intended to. But we were deceived by its sober efficiency. We believed it would do both more and less than it ought to have done. Instead it has done less and more, and brought us to many horrible passes. I suppose we would have reached these awful heights ourselves in time. And yet we have come early, and the only books we know are the ones that we ourselves wrote. They will be no help to us, just as we ourselves can be no help to each other. If someone were to forgive me for the things I did in my youth, even that would be an affront. Those crimes are the only evidence that I have lived.

I smile in greeting at a well-dressed man.
Almost immediately, he's curled in a ball
behind a rusted metal fence.

"Is that you?" I inquire. No answer.

This year's persimmon crop was poisonous.
We who know carry persimmons in our
vest pockets, and give them to mothers we dislike.

"For the children," I say. Again, the smile.

As if it wasn't enough to live in this fanciful
world, now we must touch the absurd
the way one shoves at a filthy stray,

the sort of dog that keeps tailors in business.

But oh, we are terribly kind to each other,
we are the kindest in a long line of kind hearts,
holding a door, an elevator, a place in line.

The truth is, I'm having an enormous party—

it will be a huge success. And now, if you don't mind,
I'd rather you left. All expectations to the contrary,
it seems you were not the fellow named

in this most exquisite letter of introduction.

NAMING

You are a fool, telling me the clouds are mute,
as if I hadn't heard them
talking during broad days.

They are name-givers, like the sea, their father,
saying each name once.

The wind will not forgive for this.
So it heaves them in great swells,
farther from what they know.

Left here wondering,
rolling vowels in our mouths,
what names have we been given?

Tongueless names that beckon,
even as they fade.

"Elaborations on archidiaconal themes were much sought after
in the year 900. Then commenced a bloody decade,
during which all the most famous artists and musicians
were put to death. In their wake we have seen the rise
of the Contrasouciants, the fall of the Immaterialists,
and the waxing and waning of the truer dialect
of anti-Aestheticism. However, that's not what we're
here for, that's not what we care for, is it?" asked the professor
in a knowing voice. "These midnight sessions, dangerously

arrived at, perilous in dress, tempting to the bleakest
among us: we do not come here to talk of history
or categorization. The family of man has long written
on the parchment of his own skin: 'The additions
made to life by progress and by the growths
and misgrowths of knowledge are a thorough and
insubordinable deception.' This is to say—what may be
accomplished in a single life is the matter at hand,
and the imponderable, inexpressible sentiment and

accretion of 27,000 images and the days in which they
fall—no progress can surpass what a single individual,
bent upon his own change, may do if left alone.
Thus history, the history of ages, is not the true history.
True history is simply the arc and span of your own life."
Here the professor rolled up the enormous map he'd been
referring to, and put it in a special sealed tube.
Everyone watched this operation with great interest.
"This map," the professor said, "was brought by Alexander

into the cribs and complications of many a Persian
palace. In such a palace, near long-ruined Persepolis,
Alderson Oren, the famed archaeologist, came upon it.
In my inadvisable youth, he was my sometime mentor
and left me the map when he died." One of the girls rose
and went to the window. "The rain's stopped," she said.
The others came over. Someone opened the window.
One could see in the distance, the unreal bulb of a water tower
rising out of the green-gray hills. Fog stood

in a narrow line where the river ran. From the house,
and the hill on which it rested, the farther bank
was cloaked, but the nearer was just barely visible.
"What's that?" someone asked. "What's that by the shore?"
The professor came, with field glasses, but could give no definite answer.
"It seems," he said, handing the binoculars to another,
"to be a man carrying a man upon his shoulder."
"Yes, yes," the student concurred, peering intently into the dark.
"There must have been an accident on the river."

Before dawn a light came
as if to be dawn. A man had gone

out a door, into a field. And how
he had used to go

out of a day, dog at his side.
And how he had used to fetch

crows down from blackened trees
with a good gun

and the comfort of shells.
He looked to the yards, the fields

flat with March.
He looked to the disheveled

shelf of the farmhouse roof.
And of it all, how the light

maintains upon the surface
of these things.

In a turning bore, the March Book
numbered its pages and metaphor

took no part in its sweet decisions.
The light that had grown, crept back.

The man became abstract,
absent from the field.

We will wake once, in the night;
we will recall much that must

have come before, though nothing
came before. As a dream

where long history
is written in a moment—we will rise

and retire, surrounding, surrounded,
seen in a glass from far off,

seen through a glass. In a glass
we have stood to be seen, gone

in the quiet
to places we could not understand.

And how we will wait there.
How we will wait

without sound, without sight.
Blank is the sun. Blank, all light.

2

ANNA'S SONG

Suddenly it isn't the day we thought it was.
Not the day, nor the hour, nor the season.
I am dressed in gingham, you in close-knit flannel.
There are no appointments to keep. And so I leave
My dress at the edge of this day, beside your coat and trousers,
And I say, John James,
We are circling and circling—

Come stand with me on this shadowed incline.
The grass continues, so too the trees,
So too the stream and its talk of distance.
We will not be overseen. Come lie here prone
Where my loose hands cup your name,
Where the soil is dark and difficult and cold.
I'll tell you what's to come.

THE GENERAL

Third night on the frontier:
watch fires burn as if to contain
the coming massacre. Far to the west,
by the river Ko, the sun is setting:
whose feet pace the orchard there?
Strewn like gobbets of flesh, the barbarous
flash steel: they have come to know

these plains. Even I am not certain.
Old campaigns stretch endlessly
before this old campaigner.
In autumn, from the orchard wall,
the sea is visible, unceasing.
And so I gathered men and came
here where the lines must hold.

Who among us can name his home,
can speak without fear and stand
resolute outside the haze of his own life
when the mountains come,
disguised as horsemen, sending
their weight in waves before them
shuddering over the cold ground?

AN ETCHING

Huntsmen prowl the edges of the King's woods.
One comes upon evidence of a poacher.
He calls to the next, the nearest, who turns,

gun in the crook of his arm, bright eyes narrowing.
The dogs are summoned, the horses brought.
"Winslow will catch him for sure," the men say.

"Winslow has taken an oath. Every poacher
must be hanged." The King's justice is a wild thing,
bold and curious: it sinks its teeth in ankles,

climbs into laps. It buries its nose in drink
and, overcome, makes declarations in public
that others will regret. The hounds are loosed,

the tracks followed to their terminus:
the foot of a tree. Winslow, Lord Winslow,
arrives with the foresters, and a length of rope.

"You will come down," he says, "but not,
I think, all the way." The poacher's reply
is lost to history. One can't help

but admire this crossing of lines,
this creation and guarding of lines that may be crossed
at a certain cost. One pictures the poacher's wife

watching through a window, early morning,
as her young husband passes over the yard and out
into the trees. As his hand grazes a branch,

pushes aside the arm of a bush, he's thinking
of necessities, possibilities, of the things
that he might do that day. Perhaps his passing

disturbs the forest. She'd have seen the birds rise,
and know he'd gone that way, away from the town
and toward the King's wood.

RULES

Never repeat what someone else has said,
not even in jest. Never linger in foyers,
or hang coats on chairs. Don't drink

anyone's health if the weather's bad.
Neither answer doors on the hour.
When a tree is hit by lightning, have it

made into a chair. When a man drowns
in a shattered boat, fashion the boat
into a bed. Make pillows with the down

of stolen geese. Pair your child with a swan,
and have other animals see openly
this intimate act of favoritism.

Communicate at first with letters,
though later, perhaps only in person.
Refuse to speak with distant relatives,

for they will give you nothing but mass cards
and notices of aberrant sensibility. Build
rooms in terms of the hours of day

and light and give short shrift
to well-borne-out opposing thought
on this and other crucial matters. Bide

time in alcoves, prefer hooded clothes.
Remember one building completely
and use it for memory's sake. For memory's sake,

drive slowly along the avenue of my name, and call
at every number, saying, Jesse,
there are fifteen rules for every day, and you, you fool,

you've broken every one, saying, Jesse,
we've come to take you,
we've come at last to take you where you need to go.

VOICE

In the failed township, maypoles riddle the coming of spring.
Small crowds resolve themselves, disperse.
I look on, thinking falsely,
thinking: I was once one of you.

THIS ALSO

I am walking in what appears a desert. On second thought,
it is the canal of the hopeless. I'm sure I don't belong here,

but I cut quite a figure, with my close-fitting suit,
my weighted cane, my powdered forehead.

Yes, it is a lovely day in summer. Breezes ruffle the fur
of the passing herd. As one, it makes happy stamping sounds.

In turn this pleases me, and I make a happy stamping sound.
Am I observed? Do I displease the Queen by acting so?

Yes, I know, these are the last days of an age, of a pitied era.
I'll die any day now. That's why they sent me, for a cure,

here where everyone is much smarter than everyone else,
and so no one has any peace. Driving now, with the rain,

in a cast-iron train car, I observe that someone has altered the scenery.
No longer can we look out on the world we hope for.

Comprehension comes, therefore tears. Such small mistakes
we make. It's cruel to mention them at all.

MEASURES

I took an hour in the measured water.
I left my clothing on the bank and dove

and drew my body after me.

Cautious with anger,
I took an hour

in the river water and went

six ways if I went one. The sun was
boiling on the water's surface,

and the divers sat in quiet groups

on the river floor. Their flat eyes
betrayed them, betrayed me to them,

and I could not sit long for knowing

that if I went anywhere, it was
in fear of love, and if I did a thing

that was good, if I did a great thing,

it would be in the service, in the fear of love.
And all the drowning lungs,

flopping like fish on a dock:

before the curtain of this theatre
fails beneath disgust and omen

I will find out for myself

are there any
deserving of life's reward.

AT A CROSSING

If I traveled across the unconcerned waves
and found that old path through the wood

where often prophets stood, I'd be assured

of little.
And so I am suspicious of that old path.

Therefore tell me not: you will meet
a dark-haired girl who cannot speak.

Tell me not: you will wander for days
in a stupor and arrive at a friend's threshold
at the moment of death

to watch a soul rise
along the thousandth ladder, the prime

upon which all is shuttling and weaving,

borne and bearing, as pathed as a garden,
as trafficked as a river.

FOR I have seen this friend's
soul take a quiet turning

in the space of an afternoon
and climb a distant ever-empty stair

where the apple trees are brushing
against the glass of windows

and speaking, and treating,
in the tongues of the falling.

AT DUSK

I went out, face covered, through a half-closed
door.

I went to where the boats are kept, to where
my boat is kept.

I set a hooded lantern on the rowboat's
floor,

cut strips from a blanket, to wrap
the oars.

I pushed the boat over rock, till it lay half
in water.

Two figures came, the one before
the other.

They moved down across the broken wharf,
across shore's

folded earth to where I stood,
the boatman.

I pushed the boat while two sat
on the cross plank.

I rowed the boat and the larger held
the smaller

by the throat, as we passed tiny islands,
winking in half-light.

To the deepest water, he said. It was
a long blanket,

and we both watched it sink. I rowed.
I rowed.

I pulled the boat back up across the rocks.
I watched

the larger pick his way as streams of night birds
came to docks.

3 of the 7 children, the smallest ones, of course, were starving. This meant
that the larger ones would become larger still, while the smaller would,

if anything, become smaller. Not a good situation, said Grintha,
who was listening through a keyhole. She suggests we ought to put heavy

weights on the ankles of the larger children, to give the weaker ones
a chance. Of course, I said, that might work, but that might make

them stronger. Then even we, the ones in charge, might be troubled
to make them do our will.

PASSAGE

Instruct me please so long and so well
that there will be no trouble

upon this new plain. I became
foolish with hope and crowds;

I told lies, gathered brittle ornaments.

All around, the affectionate have begun this life's work.
Their vague features and inconstant touch

are posed like questions over cabinets and keyholes
in the country of my birth. Instruct me,

if you will, for I have come upon

an easing of the way; a correspondence
has begun, as I fall in and out of sleep. I feel it:

soon I will make a language
from the grace, from the disgrace I covet,

with its sickly nature, that coughs like a child

when I throw open a window to the winter street.

ST. STEPHEN'S DAY

At the well, the invalids were cowering
under parasols, as in the distance came

the coughing of hounds.

Oh, you wrens who tremble!
intent upon nothing, useless,
flitting from weakness past grace!

Mumble on in sequestered shade.

The sun comes down; so too I'll come
around, thick smock below a scowl.

Though two get away, I'll sing and stuff eight
down the well, where new ink is made.

In the famous painting
of Giordello at the opera,
a creature is clear
behind the false forest,
just by where the costumes
would be kept. The thing
has a tail, ears like a rabbit,
and the sinuous hands of a man.
Of course, we can't know that
from the painting, which,
some say thankfully,
was lost in a flood in 1740
when Constantinople
was, for a week,
at the bottom of a lake.

The journal of the great
French master, Jacques Rennard,
has told us most
of what we know about this,
his most renowned painting.

The creature was his,
and appeared whenever he was
sketching. Most disturbing
is the rosary it seems to clutch
reflexively, in Rennard's
recollection. "It was a very
Christian beast," he wrote,
"and must be forgiven its habit
of strangling. You must understand,"

he continues, "there is a certain
grace to the strangler
that any painter must admire."

Is it coincidence that Giordello
was found, neck broken,
at his feasting table, at midnight,
the night of what Carlos Intier would call
"The Immortal Performance"?

In the last month of his life,
Rennard's maudlin fits
made his journal nigh unendurable.
One who goes that way
with fortitude will observe
on page 896, his seeming confession:
"An artist cannot live beyond
his zenith. Neither should he.
Neither ought he be allowed to."

Of course, the painting was not
complete the night of the opera,
but had only been sketched
in a long brown book Rennard
was known to carry at his waist.

"At the hour of his death,"
Beauvoir, friend to the painter,
relates, "Jacques was quite
unnerving. He slept fitfully,
occasionally sitting up straight in bed
and shouting, at impossible volume,
'I have seen this!
I have seen this to be true!'"

It seems thus that it was
generally understood
by others of that era:
either Rennard saw the creature
or was the creature himself.
As no likeness survives,
we cannot compare the two.

It seems likely he acquired the monster,
if monster there was,
during a summer stay in the tropics
when he was only a child.

HOUSE OF THE OLD DOCTOR

What is prefigured by the symbol need not be stated
baldly. The weather was bad, was dry today.
At the hospital terrible things happened
continuously. Meanwhile, the sound of gravel
in the driveway. My visitor, long overdue, arrives
with a single flower pressed in a book of riddles.
We sit on the back steps and stare wordlessly
at the ocean beside which we once lived,
which will never leave our sight. We do not stare
at the ocean. We are far from such an ocean.
It is the forest we see, shadows and the mountain
upon which the forest turns. So many animals
made wild by the dry ground. They approach the house
in darkness, and set their muzzles against the glass.
I do not think they want the things I want. By the window,
I am mouthing names: well water, carvings, apple trees.
We are near a truth, and daren't speak.

3

Manuman Notebook

I

In a braid, like weeks and days,
wedded by list, married by kind—
the limned impressions, the mind.

Differ from me, things that I do.
Be in severance, severance's pay;
watch the gated manor

where my old wants are met.
Beyond these thoughts of place,
in clean space we are seen and met.

2

The last hours of exhausted life—
we have returned to within sight of the place
where once we were born.

Captivated by folly, entranced by indifference,
what little reason we are given to smile—
is it not always enough?

At a terrible pass, the compromised
are singing "Fare Thee Well,"
invisible, like sheets of rain.

If we agree to the premise,
then mustn't we abey, mustn't we
slip sidelong to a tented place?

And if watching doesn't please us,
we must whisper a reminder of the truth—
acting, even action never frees us.

3

As if we knew, upon arrival,
that all the indulgences
were given out in decades
ended long before our births,

we made camp upon a hillside
and sat to watch the fires
take the town.

I believe you were
the prettiest of your kind,
and I never begrudged you
your ribbon, nor your fanciful air.

But we are through with
accomplishment, and gone
past all indemnity.

Our chaplain has laid out
a blanket with six knives.
He is impatient to see
how well we have shed
the costumed acts
of our second nature

4

Like cloth we rose
in momentary wind
and she was small
where small things begin.

5

A GAME OF HIDING

The parson hid in the pantry
as the children searched the other rooms
and like sardines they came
to him in the low room
one by one, a tightening grip
like a lamp or a saw blade,
like a parade ground
in the contractions of the mind.

Soon there was but one left,
the youngest child,
whose footsteps came and went
through the several rooms
in a quiet as difficult as proscription
in a weakness as binding.

6

A witness is a frail thing:
unfailing, unkempt, effete.

A broom sweeps through
these days of our inconsistence,
marking what?

        a misplaced hammer?
        a purse full of coins?
        the shadow of the chair in which you sit?

Not without reason are our long musters
ranked among the terrible, the infinite
species of learning and forgetting.

For the sound a mouth makes
is twofold—

        bent in arriving, stooped in the hall
in a corridor of doorways, each sound

is the servant not of the will alone,
not of will, but of the quieted
intents we have forgotten, that left us
at the moment of waking,

making their way, in cold determination,
along the brittle roads of our sharpest sight.

7

Don't think the consensus is arrived at easily,
for there are many golden arms
flashing beneath the sun,
many painted carts pulling by
in the thin light of a winter afternoon.

Don't calm yourself with the powder of ashes
or turn too often to an empty room,
for the sky is itself a wheel
like the graven mind, and the ground
is taut as fabric across two hands.

Which faded print will you choose,
knowing the names of days
in which it will be this across your back,
thinner than a match, this
that keeps you separate
and far from recognition
in the arms and homes of those
who without thought
would do you gravest harm?

8

With an intake of breath, the escape begins.
The frantic business of survival
indentures itself to the night.
With a glad shout we are off
into the space beyond the wall.

Who knew the cannon crash of assonance
would send our lives reeling so?
I was deceived and took
a smarter man's thoughts for my own.

But is it not always so?
A trading of selves,
a rush of blood,
a yellow cap left on the grass?

I swore our houses would be set
in a row on this darkest path,
and told you we would live
without a doubt, in grace.

Here, beyond the sentence of cordoning
or calumny, the long river motions.
We must obey.

Trees stand at the banks
lifting their pale hands.

AND what if the wind
were not a force, but a flag—

broad flag of a world

we may never see?

4

DESCRIPTION

I

In the yellow vault of antiquity, beneath
the cast hollow of pleasant hours
where we have hoped to live our lives,

a scribe is copying out the March Book.
He makes long strokes across
thin paper. He flares the intervals

of swelling words and seizes pauses
in narrow paragraphs, constricting space
with the calipers of lettered ink.

He says each word out loud
and remembers,
in sickness at the filthy

market edge, where atavistic
fragments could be bartered
and bought, his first time

reading the March Book, seeing
his name in the fragile, torn pages
and knowing he would spend

six decades copying the text.
All his daughters have left him.
One by one, they stood

at the door and called to their father.
He would not cease his work.

2

Under this sun, the March Book
spreads like another sail
raised to an ungoverned height.

It's been ages, I tell you,
beneath the ground,
where withered geography

serves for reason. The scribe
stands, pushes his chair in.
The table is empty. His mind

is flat with the weight
of process and repetition.
In a rainstorm, the March Book

crossed the sea,
though he could not follow.
Through the doorway of his hut

the land curls and ends
in water—he is thinking
and thinking still. The book

arrives on the farthest shore,
where tiny birds, too small to see,
constitute the wind,

spreading the word
of what's been done.

Though we knew that the earth was flat, yet also we knew
that our captain was in commerce with the movements
of the evening sky, and could tell all manner of fortunes
and dreams and direction, that his metal tools, carefully kept,
his astrolabe, his sextant, mustered in the closeness of his cabin,
would bring us once again to dry and solid ground.
Therefore there remained only the difficulty of dead time
and the dread of waves that is in the heart of even the greatest sailor.
On we went, on and on through starvation and the telltale lands
where misery is the keeper of joy, and not, as it is with us,
the other way around. At the edge of an arabesque, a cloud pit,
a fog, the ship stopped. There was no more ocean, nothing further.
Our captain stood beneath this display, and we could see,
like us, he was confounded. To have come all this way,
to have arrived at the very doors of a paradise beyond
all hope of recollection, and to find that simply, that truly,
our failing is that our minds are not big enough to trap
the seething pattern of the actual, that there is no sense
simple enough for these, our pathetic uses of comprehension.

FOR ONCE THE LIBERTINES DO WHAT'S BEST FOR THEMSELVES

He took the apple
and tore it in half.

She took part,
and fed it to a stray.

He gave the rest
to a swallow,
over a period of days.

These two confessed,
when they were able to
speak about the matter:

they would rather
have been left alone.

He took a tiny bell out of his pocket
and shook it three times.

Doors began to open out of trees, walls, beds, bottles.
The premises were soon crowded.

"I didn't know they lived here," Joan said meekly.
"I thought they all died in the London fire."

"Yes, well, pay up."
They went into another room.

Joan removed her skirt and blouse
and began to recite from memory

Ball's infamous Study No. 11.
"That's good," he said quietly. "That's perfect."

PARABLE OF THE WITNESS

I came to in a canebrake, covered in bruises.
"Oh, Maria," I shouted, "come carry me home!"

And there she was, that old nanny, in her patched
white nightgown, queer book of stories under her arm.

"You should have been an invalid.
What have legs ever done for you that I couldn't have?"

"Good woman!" I cried. "To candor, and to witnessing!"

We were off.

The hounds broke around us;
the mad dash drew steam. We escaped.

Oh, sorrow, seventh failure of a vaunted family,
I came to in a canebreak all alone,

and sat for hours, intent on the ground.
Never a word did I speak.

No sign there was of anyone
come to hurry me home.

LESTER, BURMA

For J.Z.

Lester and Burma were speaking gaily. He had encountered her in the hallway. Hello, he said, you certainly are a sight for sore eyes. They proceeded to a room adjoining that hall, where a large window opened onto the street. I would like to have you for supper, said Burma, and took off her dress.

I am appalled, said the doorman to the coachman, and the coachman to the gardener, at the way the young lady disports herself. You would think she had been brought up better than that.

Burma was wearing no underwear, and her slender body looked very nice on Lester's sofa. He said so. Thank you, said Burma. I swim each day, and use fine oils. Of course you do, said Lester.

What will happen, said Lester's father to Lester's mother, when that boy gets to the big city? Who will he fall in with? Will he return in ten years' time and shower us with gifts and remembrance? Or will he, said Lester's father to Lester's sickly uncle, die from the plague like all his cousins? Perhaps he will take to the sea and become a privateer, with a letter of marque. I would like that, said the uncle. I would like that also, said Lester's father.

A cloud of bees overtook the window and screened the room for a minute. Do you think they'll harm us? asked Lester. Why, no, said Burma, they're just curious. Aren't you ever curious? Yes, quite, said Lester, laying his hand upon her thigh.

The beekeeper paused by his hives. A cloud of bees is missing, he said, to no one in particular. I hope the little creatures aren't up to any mischief. I hope they return by dark so I can tuck them in their little beds and read them fairy tales.

At any rate, said Lester, we might at least have a look in the bedroom and see what's going on in there. Yes, said Burma, we might at least do that. Just to know for sure. The bedroom door closed softly behind them.

And when the bees returned to their hive, the beekeeper was there with glad tears and an admonishing word. He read them a story from a fine book he'd just bought, in which a boy and girl go to bed together with no other reason than that it is nice to be in bed with a boy and it is nice to be in bed with a girl and it is nice to wake up midway through a life in early evening to the buzzing of bees in an adjoining room.

IN PART

Sit quiet. Lie still.
Let walls stand, and windows break.
Let fires burn low.

Someone's set chairs in a circle.
Someone's wandering asleep in a cursed house.
And the joy that has its home

in the belly at the base of the soul,
let it come, let it go. Let trees be bowed
by weight, let streams race, and moss decay.

The trembling of furred limbs will not cease—
no one's word, however bold,
will banish this cold. And so, sit for no

portraits, stay for no relinquishings.
There was a moment when I was aware
of beings in the air above my head.

Have they left? Or do they loiter there,
attendant, faithful? Sit quiet,
and let the water be, let the false face

arrange itself or not, as marble basins
fill with rain, fill and empty,
empty of their own accord.

UNTITLED

The villain in the red suit
may be told to go, and he will go.

The girl who stares may be made
to turn away, and she may.

Concerns are *soluble*,
difficulties *mended*.

But this—that the tragedy of your life
may lie in wait, disguised as your life.

She told me just last night, dystrophy, saying,
"I'm a fool. I'm such a fool."

In the dream I had last night,
I drove an ambulance. Everyone

praised me, the doctors even,
for my recklessness.

In the midst of it, I left a patient
forgotten in the van.

The dream shifted;
someone had been saying,

"We're there. We're almost
there," in a comforting voice. Then silence.

I woke and realized how far I am,
how very far from the world.

The girl who stares may turn away.
The red-suited man may go, may stay.

Can't we refuse life's claims?
Isn't that what honor tells us?

I saw a speck on the horizon, moving
as if to overtake the sun. And so I say:

"In these unruly days, even prayer may be true."
Though it has never been true, in these

unruly days, let prayer be true.

The best of us have retired our skepticism
and bury letter after letter
in the salted ground of a parricide yard.

This is to say, we address the unknown
by shouting after the uncompromised.

FROM A CLEARING

I was set upon by three men.
I felled the first with a word,
the second with a blow.

Beyond them the pale city
Fortune beckoned.
But the third, oh, the third.
His face was hidden.

And in his hands he held
parchment twisted
like the bones of my throat.

MARCH HOUR

I gave the child a coin; it promised not to speak.

Beyond the shallow lake, a leak had come
through the ceiling. Paint ran, and the face

the crowd had worn was now become

wholly new. For instance, the servant girl, staid,
in severe linen, now wore her coyness like a bell.

"Remember, keep quiet!" I said, hurrying off.

If I got to her in time, she might yet remember
some past we might have had, in a nameless Welsh room.

DIAGRAM

Everyone I know is asleep right now.
I'm in a room full of strangers.
The door unlocks to admit another man
I've never seen before. It should
be morning soon, though I can't say
how long I've been here. All I know is
we've been telling lies, trying
to hurt a man we've tied to a chair
in the center of the room. He'll believe
anything. I tell him he's part
of an enormous experiment, that his wife
is a scientist and cares only for numbers.
He nods and mumbles, "I suspected
as much." Someone comes up with the idea
of keeping him in the box where we raise
flies. "He'll be uncomfortable,
I'm sure of it." Heads nod. No one knows
where the man came from, where
we came from, when we'll be allowed
to go. "I think we need to convince him
of something," says a man whose face
is entirely covered by old bandages.
"Let's use the garden hose," murmurs
someone's cruel son. "Let's shave
all the hair off his body."

In the next room, a child prodigy
is playing piano. We all strain to listen.
The man we've tied up taps his foot
in time with the music, hums the tune.
"I've always loved Ravel," he says,
to no one in particular. The old man
who holds the door grimaces, glares.
"That was Schoenberg, not Ravel."
"Quite right, I was mistaken," says the man.
"If only you knew," I said, smiling.
General laughter, then silence.

INSTRUCTIONS

Presently he happened to think
                 that perhaps what was required of him
would not be precisely
what he had been told.

He thought about that. Yes,
                 in fact, it was quite likely that
what he was told would have
very little to do with what was intended,

with what was supposed
                 to occur, and as he was the only one
working toward that end, influencing
these most particular of events, then surely

his instructions must have been
                 incorrect from the start. The question,
therefore, was twofold: one, to what end
would he have been given

a false set of instructions and, two,
                 despite all this, what should he do
in order to finish the work as planned?
He took a few steps back

and pondered the problem.
                 Of course, in a matter of minutes
another shift would start. After all,
the whole thing was the foreman's fault.

He really oughtn't do
                    more than he'd been told to.
In fact, such a deviation might
be fatal, in other circumstances.

Yes, yes, it would be best for him
                    to leave the work undone,
to walk briskly about the factory floor,
seemingly busy,

until someone else, another employee
                    in this ridiculous enterprise,
should come to relieve him. Of course,
if no one came, if no one should ever

come again, then he would have
                    no choice but to finish the work,
in whatever manner seemed possible, hoping
that by chance he would please

someone with the power to grant him
                    the sort of life he'd wanted as a boy.

An argosy, arriving at a port of call, may find
the city emptied of all save the sentinel
trees that watch over stretching avenues,

may find, stacked beyond city walls,
the famine-ridden, the dead diseased,
in piles of color.

It's then we know it's time to turn our ships around
and trail off into the trial of evening, toward home,
and hope that what we return to we will find

untouched by the pestilence of the other shore.
And our return to the home city! Our reception
at the hands of the populace. The kissing of rings,

the praising of prayer and merchant. Yet somehow
we are blamed for turning back. For it was our word
alone that named the sea impassable. Years pass.

There is now nothing to the east of us. There is
no trade. Ships rot in the harbor. Men once able
fall to dice, find themselves in afternoon, in poverty

beneath the shade of trees. Singers revel
among crowds at the shore pavilion. Watchers
on the cliff heights will see no sails. They sun

themselves on rocks and watch
for cloud banks, vast and unformed. The rain
replies with the curtaining of monotony. Silk dancers

silhouette themselves upon a hundred stages. Courtesans
with smooth shoulders stand alone in gardens. And here,
among the discarded satiates of inconclusion,

we remember the maps we once followed,
and speak of the inchoate godhead that troubled us
in the guise of tide, of fame, of fever.

A TALE

Plangent tones may string
an instrument. How then to string
a soul across the mention of these limbs?

Fables wheel in the pier glass.
The angers of small men infect
even the wells, which center,

cruciform now, on festivals of birth.
Carlos, I have devised a method
by which to build the place

in which I may be happy.
It is difficult, involves altitude
and the early afternoon. A maypole,

a wharf: set against
gray morning in the freight of spring.
What I am told I want

I do not want. This is how
one begins to be happy, by leading
a slow trail through the brazen

chorus of disbelief. The routed
are running still, on an immense hillside
beneath a single yellow cloud.

We are speaking now
at the hill's edge, where crooked trees
conceal our ugliness.

Do you hear me? We are the routed.
There are no others. Upon our arms,
the scars of proscription. Within our

lifeless eyes, the stamping out of fire.

PROBLEMS OF WARFARE

Lindy tells me another one has washed ashore.
It's late afternoon, but there's light yet,
so we walk down to have a look. And here,

she says, is his helmet. And here, his canteen.
He had no gun, or rather, if he had it, it must
have been lost along the way. The soldier

peers up at us, hostile and weak. Lindy laughs
and throws a bit of sand in his face. This makes
the soldier flinch, and one can see he's trying

to bring his arm up. Of course,
we can't have that. So Lindy and I, we set
to clubbing the soldier, I with my heavy

stick, she with a rock tied up in cloth. He's
the third in a week, soon weaker from our treatment
than he was from the sea. "Depart!" I shout, "Fail!"

and strike him heavily in the temple so his face
crumples in a wrong way. I can tell his skull
won't bear up much more. Snuffling sounds

come unbidden from the cavity
of his nose and mouth. But we shall stay
to hear no words.

Now, Lindy, Lindy dear, let's head up the hill
and have our supper. The dogs will find their way
and finish this, such as it is, tonight.

A calliope? A room in the house where I
was born? I was never told. Don't think

your attendance at some latter-day unveiling
gives the lie to much of anything. A cipher

is second to last in any number of wild lists
made with you in mind. And besides,

I'm starting to recall chords of pure volume,
wide as the principal avenue in some

unquestioned history. If it was not my name
it was the beginning of my name, a word said

slowly, long ago, having in mind
the whole of this, the entire plain of featureless

days, and how they figure in the play of nerves
across an uncomposed face.

PRAIRIE HERMITAGE

Trappists with beveled faces neglect the lower rooms
of this old house in which they shelter. God keeps
to the rooftops in our town, where men are known
by silhouettes of sun-blanched feature, women
by the motion of fans. Here we are not often called upon
to attend to bells, or to the clarion of visiting voices.

A hundred years ago, when the prairie was the fact
of this place, the Felk brothers, barbers,
were hanged among the limbs of the Great Oak
that presides over New Trafalgar Square.
They were highway robbers, apprehended in their guise
as ordinary men. As such they died.

From this house of worship, the scene opens
with a monk gesturing, calling though not speaking,
as a terrible wind musters in the eastern reaches of the sky.
For weeks a thousand mile storm has grown closer.
It's clear we shall wake tomorrow to weather as it was
before men knew the causes of the world.

5

Several Replies in a
Numbered Column

One does not need to be an aerobatic artist or a trick shooter;
rather, (one has) to have the courage to fly right up to the opponent.

—Manfred von Richthofen,
Der rote Kampfflieger, Berlin, 1917

I   *And if there were arguments in the house where I lived, then I was conscious only of argument. I sat, listless, on the quiet stairs, mouthing violent phrases, swearing myself to vanished causes and collapsed moments. I could bear this, because I have a stolid face and a grasp of games. I was involved in a lie so deep that nothing could be proven, not by me or by anyone I knew. All basis for deduction was nonexistent. And so I could let words stream from my mouth, in a hundred misplaced contexts.*

It gets easier, the longer I speak, for you to recognize what's false, what's mine, what's made. I recognize as I trace the silhouettes of famous scabs. There's something in a nose that makes a man cross a picket line. I'll never cross. Scraped-up knuckles, torn trousers, scratched boots. It's only a fight if there's a good chance you'll lose.

And so we remain the best of friends, you and I, strolling haphazardly across parks, through districts. I point to the mountains that loom beside this northern city, having sat atop them, having sat atop mountains and felt that if the sky threatened rain, then it was I who was threatening.

It's terrible to think I give, never to know how it will fare with you. Here's my hope that you'll have strings to tie up all the trees. Here's my hope that I find you at your best, crouched beneath a withered sun, among the last, glad to hear any news, even news as poor as this.

·

33   What was lovely remained lovely. All the vestiges of last week's rain were present in the smallest gesture, a turn of a slim wrist, the catcall intonation of voices heard at distance, saying things we knew once to be true. They are true still, but not for us, so we must search these landscapes for new truths, and what was once the guide will be a guide no longer. There was a scene I saw once in a film—I was passing through a room in early evening, eager to be on to what was next, but I recall the faces of the famous man and woman and how they stood. Were they exiled in a foreign place with sand for trees, the sun in place of seasons? It seemed so, and I took that with me as I left the room, took off across the evening city. These are clues to how I chose to make my life, these faces, not yours, not mine, but how I wished they were, how I wished our lives were patterned on those lives that were best led before. It seems false that we must make the same mistakes again and again. I had been sorry long years before you took my hands and led me through the falling snow to your three rooms on the edge of town. I would call for that again, no comfort save as satiate to an endless pain. Administer yourself to me as though I were the boy you met in a dream of some possible future. You told me of it once, clear eyes and the palest skin. He led you to a lake, removed your clothes; he pulled you in. What could be softer than those waters?

Not this, not this, but my heart, but the grinding of days, and my heart in your hands.

.

67 And though the words of my friendliness are not false, they may easily seem false, they may easily function falsely in many of the worlds in which they appear. I was gaunt and pale, a stranger with a hunger for things that were not present in my day. And so I spoke of those things, and called for them. Though I loved the places in which I sheltered, though hospitality was the name and signal of my protector, still I spoke of what was lacking in my heart, and others, seeing it to be lacking about them, and in them as well, took their landscapes and their homes as false, and went looking elsewhere for sincerity, sincerity having then grown to be what was lacking, though never would I have said, arriving, that what was present within each hold was false. I was a lover, of nothing living and nothing dead, and what I loved had not yet, perhaps would never come to pass. Yet it seemed but distanced from me by this wall, by that door. Should I win the heart of she, or he, should I drive a stake into cold packed earth and make a place to live my life . . . each thing became less as soon as it became. It was years before a first tentative step could be taken toward any comfort. Such years are not remembered. Such seriousness is compelling to thought but not to memory. Days when we can see our lives stretched out in all directions, they are themselves ciphers, altitudes on a flat

map, as lines verge on the obvious, then fall again into hazy misapprehension.

.

99   To move your hand just so, and conjure for an audience that is always being born. A poet can afford few tricks, for he is easily seen through. Whole generations may be warned against him, and still he beguiles those more willing, those who see because they care to, because it is their freedom to accept what others discard, to populate dead roads with the living who wander, one question on their lips. And have you been fooled? And will you be fooled again? I laid a trail in the daybreak woods with the carcasses of tiny animals, each of whom loved me well. And I was sad to do this, but there was grayness to the light, and the killing seemed correct. What if the trail ends in underbrush, no answer but the crushing weight of hot air in the lungs? Where would you go next? Where else would you go looking for the inspiration that's driven each night through your skull with a hammer the size of your life? And there are questions leading on to questions. . . . Who could lift such a hammer, who would and why? There are reasons only in so much as we have need of them, and surely you can see, we have no need to know the origin of things. If I were a madman, scratching statements in the sides of trees with rusty clippers found beneath my bed, why, I would write a hundred things I had no business knowing, and my business in

knowing them would be the life of madness. What we drove home that night, what we drove before us with the force of our intentions, was a spirit that was living alone in the hills but that now lives off the heat of your breath, the factory of your limbs. I had a mind to tell you, when we played the cloud game and lay for hours inventing—well, I could not see the clouds for anything but clouds. Yet I could see your mind, and your thoughts, and I could tell them to you before you ever knew that they were yours. How we were in love that day, and thinking there was nothing for it but to name a place to which we might escape. Well, we have escaped. What names will we give ourselves now? We may build a fire that is so large that there is no standing about it, but only standing in it, and we will watch it take us, and we will watch it take all that we know, and we will call this fire the happiest time of our life, and it will be our life, but we will not be living it. We will have lived it. We will look back upon the living of it. The things we cannot anticipate are so pale in memory. I was struck by a car, hurled through the air, and I do not remember. I was a child then, living beside a road. Many years have passed.

.

156   And who can weather the contingencies of belief, emerging to say, I know why I believe what I believe? There are few such, and I am certain that they do not speak, or if they do, they do not speak to me. It is not for them I write

these lines, not for them I make an empty place at table. And it is not for you, though you may sit there at table, though you may read all I write and say, may know what I know, have what I have. Say this to yourself, there have been casualties in this life, who will not see what I have done, who are gone off now to compose the world that I love, to make of themselves the very wind that comes of an afternoon when everything living resounds, and everything dead sings in empty echo. Say this and know that my belief is true, without knowing why; join me in the passing of columns along an empty grass run road, and act if you can, for properly, there is no audience to be a part of, and so you are no part of it. Forced to the stage, make no complaint about the hour, about your lack of preparation, your untrained tongue. For the tongue is trained to itself, and taut with force of mind, and what you have to tell can truly be lost and never heard again.

We are a species, a splash in the waters of a land-bound lake, and we may speak in turn, as long as we may, and when we are finished there will be no one to speak, or hear, or write, or dream. It is of consequence to note the passing moments, the manners of our days. Allegiances and hands are held in the chambered heart, and it is filling itself, shuddering great arcs of light, of blood, of liquid so heavy with animate that it makes us ourselves to move, and moves us to thought. "To thought? Toward what?" mumbles the chorus, in vague dissent. A row of trapeze artists in an empty theater, who rock slowly on a central beam, they disagree. It is their slow rocking that troubles me most, and the awkward angles their knees assume, their elbows take: such figures are proof of something. It is not given yet to know of what.

·

201 But do not fail me—for even now I hear my name being called. I turn, arm still stretched by the small demands of bandages, practically wrapped, as at first, with a torn dress. We've been through this. No one's calling. I'm asleep on a bench, and it is forbidden to be outdoors between the hours of 8 and 9. It is forbidden to be curious about the hours of 8 and 9. It is forbidden to mention them.

All of these tricks I employ may be wasted. It's easy to see oneself under one's own spell. But I'm sure you duck better than I. I'm sure you've seen me coming, the length of the street. (Determined, with wild hair, narrowed eyes.) My eyes are always narrowed. It is the narrowing of myth, and helps me to make out some hoped-for importance in the hunching of men, in the Saracen mathematics of which we claim control.

·

219 But mastery, as we know, is the act of the desperate. One doesn't need it if one has flowers, a pinafore, a carved toy, a jackknife and trees to hand.

I've spent decades beneath low ceilings just to
learn vowels, sounds that may be used to warn.
Much that I needed has passed away, and with
it the need. Being human means *continue*.
Quiet ghosts kneel behind doors wherein the
pledges they once held are daily broken. And
I? I have been given cause and speak. Such a
curious gift—it hurries the passage of time,
and makes consequent the factories of roads,
foundries in which the weight of our footsteps
was once predicted.

.

234   You were with me in those years before the
century turned. Season after season of
indolence, the play of voices against boughs of
leaves. The world was screened by a world
made of cloth, painted with the faces of the
people I knew. It could be parted with a hand,
with a gesture, but this was a thing little
known. And so we grew fond, and made no
gestures, and saw in this cloth world fortnights
expire and stretch uselessly on the garden
steps. And when the party had passed down
those long steps from the solarium, we two
were left behind, peering down over the west
wall into the kennels built below. There was
disorder in the air. The dogs were passing back
and forth at the base of the wall, scrambling on
each other's shoulders and scraping at the
stone. I said, half to myself: There will be an
end to this, that we have always known. A
messenger came at dusk, and what we know,
the dogs know. They point like a needle and

show us the weather that rises even now, in the deep places beyond the hills. This gathering of things beyond sight—it is my future.

My hands shook then, as they always have, as they still do, and my clothes were simple, but there was no death in me. What could I have said to preserve that season? What vowels could have moved us to a new delight? If I sometimes dream of a life without poetry, then it is a false dream. I am lucky to wake in this body, lucky to wake in this time. Lucky to wake with you beside me, listening still.

.

267   On film the mummer's dance seems lethal. Against the sky planes hardly move. Context both obscures and abuts meaning. Difficulty pinions hope. Hope is meaning. I woke every day for a week with an image in my head: a ring of trees, a picnic, a sundress. I've bought the wine, I've listed the perishables. The cloth is folded on a side table. Spring reflects itself in shop windows, in the warmth of stoops. Like kissing, it seldom is what it is. Like prayer, it has an object. Like instinct, it's a thing of skin. Each spring I say to myself: The winter is kindness, the spring is grief. We are loveliest when grieving, buoyant in the salt of a water that stings at wounds, that does its best to drown us in the foreignness of a substance that once was familiar. Equally, we choose to keep it present. We leave the city and take a room in an empty town, just to walk the beach

at dusk. Under a seat in the old opera house, we may find, if luck is with us, a tiny golden ball. Though it is not the sun, it is similar, and dangerous in the same way.

.

290 If there were seven, then I was the eighth, not wholly present, disputed, unarrived. Doors were barred. Windows were locked. And the girl who loved me loved the space beside her in the bed, though it went unfilled, night after night. When I went to claim it, it was there still, and fit me cleanly, taut to my every muscle. It was my place and bent when I bent, sang when I sang. What makes the fire run from house to house? In moments half the city is ablaze, and flocks have risen to the sky. There is room yet for you in comprehension of fire, of wind, room yet for you in the watching. Those who counted may not have thought of you. Yes, they have left you out, they have overlooked you. They do not know this better way with numbers that says: I am nine, though there are ten present, though I am not present; that says; I am the origin of numbers, and of numbering, and mine is the final count. Never believe admission can be denied. Admit what you will, letting gentle breezes through the open door. The hat shop is madness. Certain birds love raw meat. In the dawn, the report of a poacher's gun travels far. If I, out taking the air, heard such a sound, I'd never tell. We who carry broken watches as if

they were sound—we have a contract kept in a hidden place. We will keep it there awhile.

.

319   What does it mean to be adored? All of the table settings have gone astray, and yet we are striving to prepare ourselves for supper. The door to the street is open, and though it is summer, I am forced to ask myself, "What is summer, what is a thing for which I have waited so long?" There is no food in the pantry, just empty shelves. The flicker of motion in the street—someone is going home. But you are less able than they. You are at home. And the terror of the minute hand, the long failure of hours, the discrepancy of seconds in the mind: they are the only contributors to a song that sings like a vacuum in your head, a rush of air followed by pain. What we want is to be rescued, but when we are ourselves we are ornate, far too heavy to be carried. If you left the door open, then you hoped for the uninvited guest, the one who may give warmth as the fire does not. I have seen him crossing the open spaces, simply attired, moving with a sureness that was staggering. I did not follow him; I could not bear to see what that arrival would be like, when he has spurned my door and scorned my table, when he has walked through the wood beside my house each day of his infinite life, each day of my infinite life, and has never come calling on me.

349   Served at table by men and women, each more
lovely than the last, served dishes and courses
that ebb on for hours, served liquors in
fashions that dim light and day, I retire for a
moment to the street, leaving the laughter of
company. I know then that I am a plain man.
Geometry is my science, the method of
arriving at a thing by staring it into sense. A
girl passes in the street, alone, and though there
are girls for me in the place from which I came,
I want this girl because she is alone. Surely she
knows what it is like to be on the street and see
me—surely she thinks that because I am alone
I too resist the quiet by singing beneath my
breath. It's true, I want to say. You're right
about everything. We are the thousand
variations. We project ourselves on every
wall. We don't need shadow. We don't need
light to manage it.

And so she passes, and I return to the meal,
which is grander with each moment. Night
ends in a bed. It begins with a stripping of
sheets. When I go down to the morning and
the morning street I am amazed again.

The fascination morning holds is that it is
always cleaner, more complete, than we
imagine.

•

376   When the dead leave paper, it is best used
without malice. Even the hint of a grin can

bring the tragic on wide wheels like a summer-day parade. Everyone's tending to flower boxes. Everyone's opening mail. The Dutch door depends upon the farmyard; one day both will be extinct. In a district of churches, I sketch you with the ease of a master. The drawing itself is less gifted. It will go in a trunk, to be looked at on two occasions before I die.

.

386 *And so, you see that what I told you on Tuesday, when we lectured each other in the rain, when we sprang upon the back of that great stone lion and his twin, whispering apocryphal details, spouting inconsistencies, now you see that I was lying.* I told you then that I would care to know, really, which particle was the smallest, and how fast it moves, and all the other sundry details that go to explain everything save the need for explanation itself. Believe me, I love the quest for this particle. I love late hours in the laboratory, when the atomic rain has fallen in tiny happy chambers, duly recorded, noted in a spidery hand on paper sheets produced expressly for that and no other purpose. Gladly I will creep about in such a place, exchanging niceties with those researchers who labor, deep inside the human cell. They love their mining, and I love them for loving their mining. But I am no miner.

IF the lion bucked, and his replica rose sphinxlike in our esteem (speaking all languages, knowing the wisdom of ancient gods), then we were amazed, and that was enough.

I have been a passenger on a yellow ship that any doubt would founder. And so, I am grateful to tell whatever occurs and the manner of its occurrence. And here and now, what occurs is this thought, this striking of nerves. And so I tell it, speaking my mind as though it were a map of the greatest of cities, made long before your birth, a thing that your life cannot question, because the questioning and the rebuttal have gone their separate ways, leaving you a simple yes, a simple movement of the eye along the page.

．

423   There were men who named the crowds and called to them at need. These men cared not for who composed the crowds, cared only for the energy with which these currents ebbed and flowed. And though I am intimate with this verse, though I know the feel of it beneath my hands, I know it only as men have known the crowd. For it is unfamiliar to me in ways, and seems to each new observer as it will never seem to me. A man shouts, points a finger. The crowd ascends a wall, to stand upside down upon the ceiling and chat of strangeness. A man shouts, points a finger. The crowd surrounds a child, steps into his heart, steps into his limbs, inhabits well and long his head, puts cloth across his eyes. I was afraid of these things once—that there is no control for

speech, nor over speech, nor in speech itself. And so I ready myself with contradictions, and give you this view and that, and this idea backwards compounded by rumors on the x axis that the land to the west is populated only by liars.

As though conclusions were the point of anything . . . we shall all come to the same conclusion. Let us live on cliffs among the filthy seabirds, and scavenge eggs from hidden nests. The only thing worth disguising has already been disguised.

.

452   The palpable was a myth that we knew better than to laugh at, for were our shapes not bent beneath the weight of a thousand gravities that would never relent? Count yourself among those situated upon a high place. Let this elevation speak to you and bring to your senses details long lost even to the wise.

.

How shall I intermingle my blood and my worth with the mass that crawls in the alleys and lanes? I have heard that question, long posed on your lips. And you will hear it posed again and again, at each crossroads, each waking from occupation. Only the very old, on the eve of death, have played their hand so thoroughly that they are left with no recourse. Bend your mind to this better philosophy— that everything that is is in the service of your senses, and that your love is the equal to the love of the world. Could you call it forth, you would believe me. But you must believe first, without counting scope or merit, without thought of safety. There is no safety. Everything is visible, and everything is harmed, and everything is waiting to be harmed again.

.

476   At that the door is shut firmly from within, and we are left in the hall with a sinking feeling. Was there something more? There was not, I say quietly. You nod, your stern young face upturned, and we return to the stairs that lead down to our many and varied destinations, each taxing us a little more, until we too grow old, until we too are visited in the unrecognizable depths of our age, when such a door as the one upon which we knocked today will open and then close in evening. One of us will be behind it, the bent one who turns in to the room, unsteady feet upon a faded carpet, who makes his way toward a row of gabled windows to lock them shut, each one, against the coming of night.

And if there are questions then, gathered in the cotton of our bedsheets, draped among the dusty remains of the piled things that we chose one by one, then they are not pressing. For how could they be? How could they be of any importance? If they were, would we not have asked them long before, in our youth or in our prime, when our minds were agile, still capable of understanding whatever answers might be offered? No, these questions are not pressing. They are merely old questions, long answered, now risen again in confusion. Beg for the answers if you must, but beg them only of yourself. Beg them only to pass the time.

.

506   Oh, but do not take me at my word. For how could I, who prize this life for what it is—a single egregious question—ever speak of failure, ever say there is a time when one who wishes to think may not be able to think. Or worse, that I should say such attempts are worthless. No, no. I talk only of what I fear. You know me, you know of me: a coward, a gambler. For my skin will be no help to me in this struggle with the opaque. And though I have the marks of a proud family etched variously on my frame, I fear even this. To speak of my cowardice and thus make it real. Well, it has always been real, with or without my consent. Consent has had no part in this life.

.

522   There was a time when I stood by the barber amid a crowd of arguing men. I proclaimed that the world has always been precisely the way it is now. "Progress is an illusion for the weak-minded," I shouted, and others took up the cry. But there was one, in the back of the room, who quietly rebutted my every word.

He did this simply and without an audience, and when I was done speaking, during the clapping of backs and hands, he slipped out the rear. He knows all the back ways and all the arguments, and they are all, he will confide, in one tedious vein. He is pleased not by relative merit, but only by impetus. It is this study of moments— of how a thing is caused—that is his greatest love. "The universe has not yet been created," he is fond of saying. "Nor will it ever be."

.

539   In the counting houses, the counting has stopped. In the bell tower, the ropes have frayed, the ropes have snapped. The bells are falling through masonry, weight following weight. With each moment, a new note is struck. Never mistake the world's inanimacy for purpose. Purpose is a human trait, bred in ice-age migrations, endless winters, feral springs. The notation you see in scholarly books, left open on a table, in a library's ancient wing, where the steps you take have long been apprehended, commented upon, discarded—it is no cause for worry. It must be true: men have lived and died happily. Yet these accounts are missing from the annals. For now you see—the glad don't trouble themselves with certainty. This is how a mirror becomes a door. This is how a letter arrives, smuggled, at a crucial hour. The urgency of hospitals, of necessary truth, is inconceivable on this hot day, when the grass is *growing*. Everywhere, ants well up out of

loose soil, intricate, manifold, working toward an end. How can there be so many? How can there be ten million ants to counter every human mind? Ten million ants, carpeting the ground, in a field to which you will never go.

.

566   Is there a distance more profound than the distance of oneself from one's own observations, when separated by time? To know something truly, completely, and to be the genesis of insight, and then later, days, weeks, years later, to look upon that thought as on a foreign city, where populations have borne lives without number to which you were never party, though perhaps you knew their father's father, or his father's father before him. The blood has grown thin, and the streets are quite unrecognizable. The myriad paths of our feet and our body through life, drawn out on a map, some small infinity of repeated passage, is as nothing to the courses of the mind, which moves as even Mercury cannot, bridging impossibilities with assertions of the possible born of misunderstandings that in time become truth. Poetry may list, may render records in this archive of my mind's long tale. I was born in a village by the sea, in a place of widow's walks and barbershops. A man in cold colors stood with a beard at the shore and told me, this dream, this one apart from all others, it is your life, and though others may form and fail, this thread has weight unlike that which will follow, and unlike that which came before. You will

never know these things to be true, for your movement between such states will be indistinguishable. Say that the grass has passion. Say that it once was born as you, to walk upon the land, and that when the universe is cold, and all matter distant from all other matter, then that will be our longest sleep.

.

600   Artists mimic the objects of our lives with great precision. Some contrive worlds where you may live despite your separate, outer life. Still others make a badge of their difference, and disclude you from the products of their work. I am not of these types. I am a machinist, and I build theatres, and in those theatres I say the most foolish things I can think of. I do not, of course, think at the time that these things are foolish. At the time I am in love with the substance of my thought. It seems to me, in this haze, that every inch of existence is carpeted in a rich substance. To touch anything is divine, et cetera, et cetera. And then I am ashamed to have said so to a full house.

But this shame can be borne, and it is a bright and pleasing existence, building chutes and passages for thought. Acrobats enlist and sign their paychecks with an X. I employ only the illiterate, as I hate when what I write is read from over my shoulder. Wait until I speak! I shout. And my lovely legions wait, and talk of things in the clear autumn light. It's early evening, and supper will be soon. Geese make numbers in the sky, and the light doubles them softly upon the ground. We are all ancient, and no one has seen half so much as we have seen. No one has left to see half so much as we have left to see. And though I will die, it is of no importance. For the air is temperate here where I make my home, and the dusk is gentle, and when morning comes I will go walking in long fields while the earth sleeps fitfully, beneath leaves as opaque, as delicate, as crumbling as my own memories and the faces around which they pulse and gather.

NOTES

The epigraph, "But now thou dost thyself immure and close/ in some small corner of a feeble heart" is from the poem, "Decay," by George Herbert.

"#31, Conflict With a God" refers to the thirty-first of 36 possible dramatic situations.

"From a Clearing" was written initially on a bedroom wall in a house in Bedford Stuyvesant.

The writing that is visible in the lower left hand corner of the Brueghel drawing has been translated as "He who knows where the nest is, knows it; he who has the nest has it." (An old Dutch proverb).

ACKNOWLEDGMENTS

This book could not have made its ungainly appearance without the help of others. I'd like to thank Catherine Ball for her continued and indefatigable support. To Richard Howard and his eagle eye I owe a huge debt. Others who deserve thanks are: Glyn Maxwell, Lindsay Sagnette, Rob Reddy, Eamon Grennan, Todd Jones, Tim Kindseth, Liam Rector, Paul Russell, Stacie Cassarino, and Jana Zabinski.

As well, I am thankful for the munificence of the Red Barn in Michigan.